MW00389281

This book belongs to:

____

67137992R00065

Made in the USA
Columbia, SC
23 July 2019